YOUR KNOWLEDGE HAS VALUE

- We will publish your bachelor's and
  master's thesis, essays and papers

- Your own eBook and book -
  sold worldwide in all relevant shops

- Earn money with each sale

Upload your text at www.GRIN.com
and publish for free

Anna Leiber

Italy's first steps towards a new Europe (1945- 1957)

GRIN Verlag

Bibliografische Information der Deutschen Nationalbibliothek:

Die Deutsche Bibliothek verzeichnet diese Publikation in der Deutschen National-
bibliografie; detaillierte bibliografische Daten sind im Internet über http://dnb.d-
nb.de/ abrufbar.

Imprint:

Copyright © 2014 GRIN Verlag GmbH
Druck und Bindung: Books on Demand GmbH, Norderstedt Germany
ISBN: 978-3-656-82125-0

This book at GRIN:

http://www.grin.com/en/e-book/282699/italy-s-first-steps-towards-a-new-europe-
1945-1957

Italy's first steps towards a new Europe -

Political Developments between 1945 and 1957

Table of content

„Italy is ready to transfer wide powers
to a European Community, provided that it
be democratically organized and give
a guarantee of life and development."

Alcide De Gasperi,
Italian Prime Minister (1945-1953)

1. Introduction

In 2007, the European Union celebrated the 50th anniversary of the Treaties of Rome, and thus its official hour of birth after many years of intensive negotiations, which had lasted from 1945 till 1957. From the very beginning on, Italy "had been amongst the keenest supporters of the European integration, both at the popular and the government levels" (Comelli 2011: 2) and had played an important role within all early proceedings. Especially under the political leadership of Alcide de Gasperi, Italy became one of the most influential negotiators and until today, the country is considered a triumphant founding nation of the European Union (Di Nolfo 1980: 145). This widespread pro-European attitude, however, has declined dramatically during the last decades.

Although nowadays - in a time of expeditious global developments, growing mutual dependencies and uncertainties - the "European integration seems more essential than ever" (Dinan 2005: 7), Italy's opinion about a European future changed for the worst. Two factors mainly led to this negative development: Silvio Berlusconi's Euro-sceptical government during the so-called Second Republic as well as the disastrous financial crisis in 2008/2009 (Comelli 2011: 8). As recent surveys considerably show, the Italian population has lost its originally belief in the European Union. Many people demonstrate against strict austerity programs, consider Europe as a danger for the national future and fear a steady weakening of the Italian political and cultural heritage (Caciagli 2004: 26). Looking at the following results of a Europe-wide survey conducted by an American political research centre between 2007 and 2013, the waning position of the European Union among the Italian population is evident. Whereas in 2007 78% of the Italians still looked favourably at the European Community, the picture changed dramatically till 2013. By then, only 58% of the people shared a positive opinion about the united Europe. Although Italy's result in 2013 is still the second best after Germany, the immense downfall of the Italian favourability shouldn't be disregarded. Especially concerning the fact that "Italians – elite and public alike – were once amongst the most Europhile people in Europe" (Comelli 2011: 2).

2

EU Favorability Waning

% Favorable

	2007 %	2009 %	2010 %	2011 %	2012 %	2013 %	*07-13 Change*
Spain	80	77	77	72	60	46	*-34*
France	62	62	64	63	60	41	*-21*
Italy	78	--	--	--	59	58	*-20*
Czech Rep.	54	--	--	--	34	38	*-16*
Poland	83	77	81	74	69	68	*-15*
Britain	52	50	49	51	45	43	*-9*
Germany	68	65	62	66	68	60	*-8*
Greece	--	--	--	--	37	33	*--*

PEW RESEARCH CENTER Q9f.

Source: PEW Research Center (2013)

This negative relationship between Italy and the European Union, however, might be recovering from now on. Matteo Renzi, who got elected the new Italian prime minister in February this year, seems willing to contribute decisive activities to move the Italian population again closer to Europe. As a first important step, Renzi used his government declaration to underline the historical significance of the European Union and the urgent necessity for Italy to restart European cooperation (N24.de 2014). Referring to his prominent political precursor, Alcide de Gasperi, the Italian prime minister promised to close the gap between Italy and Europe again.

Picking up this recent look back to the founding period of the European Union by the Italian prime minister, this paper focuses on exactly that time and analyses Italy's contribution during the early European integration. Political scientists and historians often divide this process in three main parts: the after-war period between 1945 and 1949, the beginning of multilateral negotiations from 1949 till 1954, and finally the most important time for the European unification ending with the ratification of the Treaties of Rome in 1957 (Di Nolfo 1980: 148).

In the subsequent analysis, I will follow this structure and thereby concentrate on the most decisive events that took place within the different periods - first and foremost the Brussels and Atlantic Pact (1948), the Schuman Declaration (1950), the European Defence Community (1952), the Spaak Committee (1955), and the Treaties of Rome (1957).

2. 1945 - 1949: Italy's situation after the Second World War

"In the immediate aftermath of the war, Italy's predominant need was a period of recuperation – to build a new political system after twenty years of Fascism, to reconstruct the economy from the ruins of the war, and to regain a position of equality internationally. Only when these tasks had been completed could Italy think again about Europe." (Willis 1971: 13)

As in many European countries, the Second World War had left disastrous marks in Italy. The political as well as the economic infrastructure was destroyed, great parts of the population were homeless and unemployed, and the people suffered from hunger, illnesses and traumata.

In December 1945, Alcide de Gasperi was elected prime minister. His first cabinet governed until July 1946 and tried to use this short period to stabilize the Italian political system as much as possible (Willis 1971: 14). Also during his second ministry, where de Gasperi kept the Ministry of Interior in order to have a better control about the restoration process, the coalition parties focussed mainly on the national economic reconstruction (Daniels 1998: 107). Building any international relations was unthinkable at that time due to the severe inner state problems.

The Italian government soon realized, however, that it needed foreign support to successfully re-erect the country. Therefore, it addressed itself to the American government in order to gain some financial aid. In the context of the Marshall Plan, Italy got finally supported and, by the end of 1947, the national production "was approximately at the level it had been in 1938" (Willis 1971: 15). Having stabilized the economic condition, de Gasperi wanted to improve Italy's international status as fast as possible. In his opinion, it should be the most urgent goal for the Italian nation not only to reach an inner state situation of normality, but also regarding the international connections. His wanted to show the other nations that Italy was a country like the other states - with the same rights and obligations, the same international relations and the same rules for diplomatic behaviour (Di Nolfo 1980: 151).

Regarding the rising tension between the USA and the UDSSR, De Gasperi tried to stay neutral towards both superpowers. The US government, however, informed the Italian prime minister in 1947 that the "continuance of aid to Italy was dependent upon maintenance of a stable democratic system at home" (Willis 1971: 18). It was therefore obvious that the USA would only continue to support Italy as soon as members of the Communist Party didn't hold any political positions anymore. De Gasperi reacted immediately to this official warning from the American side and formed a new government, his fourth cabinet, composed only by Christian Democrats and three independent ministers (Di Nolfo 1980: 146). With this reaction, de Gasperi left his neutral comfort zone and showed a major commitment to the American alliance.

Within the following year, the question about Italy's position towards the United States determined the political discussions between the opposition and the governing party. It therefore became the main campaign topic during the elections in April 1948. Whereas the Communist and Social Party considered the Marshall plan and any other cooperation with the American side as a great danger for Italy, de Gasperi and his cabinet underlined the importance of such means for Italy's future (Willis 1971: 21). De Gasperi won the elections and saw his pro-American and international orientation publicly acknowledged. As he was an enthusiastic proponent of international cooperation, he used his new election success to bring Italy and its European neighbour countries closer together.

A first important step towards any unification with other European countries was Italy's bilateral cooperation with France – the Franco-Italian customary union. In 1948, de Gasperi, his foreign minister Sforza and the new elected French foreign minister Robert Schuman decided upon this common project. Although the cooperation mainly focussed on an economic interchange between the countries, Sforza as well as Schuman saw it also politically as "the real beginning of the union of Europe" (Willis 1971: 21). Within the same year, in March 1948, France constituted the framework of another European alliance. Together with Britain and the Benelux countries it signed the Brussels Pact, which led to the military cooperation named Western European Union. The Italian government, however, showed no interest in joining this alliance. De Gasperi and Sforza were aware of the population's uneasiness towards any military obligation. After the disastrous events of the Second World War, the Italians feared that any kind of military cooperation might be followed by future conflicts (Di Nolfo 1980: 162). This neutral attitude soon provoked a strong irritation on the American side.

The US government wanted to build another military alliance together with Canada and the Brussels Pact countries, the so-called Atlantic Pact, and it officially requested de Gasperi and Sforza so that Italy would join the Pact. As Italy was still dependent on the American financial support, de Gasperi knew that in order to stabilize the international relations with the United States as well as other European countries, his country had to be responsive to the American pleas. Although they both know how critical the Italian population was towards this cooperation, de Gasperi and Sforza considered the Atlantic Pact to be a possible cornerstone for a successful European unification:

"On one hand European union increases the solidarity of the Pact, while the Pact supplies the union with the necessary shield behind which it can survive and develop. On the other hand, the union assures (…) the independence of the European states which, associated together, will constitute an entity capable of autonomy in face of the United States." (Willis 1971: 26)

3. 1949 - 1954: From the Schuman Declaration to the European Defence Community (EDC)

The second important period within the early European integration was shaped by the close collaboration between Italy and France and the reappearance of a German national state. When the Federal Republic was founded 1949, "most Italians looked upon it with the same distrust and foreboding as the French did" (Willis 1971: 32). The memories of the German policy during the Second World War were still present in both countries. In order to set up a future international control over the German war industry and, at the same time, to integrate the new German state in a supranational political alliance, Robert Schuman proposed an important framework in 1950, the Schuman Declaration. The main goal of this plan was to unify the French and German production of coal and steel and to put it under a common high authority. By that, so Schuman's idea, any military confrontation between France and Germany became impossible. In order to embed this foremost military idea into the ongoing process of the political and economic European integration, Schuman gave also other European countries the possibility to participate.

Although de Gasperi was glad about the reconciliation of the two countries, he soon feared a "Franco-German hegemony in western Europe" (Willis 1971: 33). Therefore, he decided to participate in the Schuman Plan and to act as a mediator between France and Germany. In April 1951, the treaty was signed and created the European Coal and Steel Community (ECSC). What looked on the first glance as only an economic alliance focussed an ambitious political goal: the Coal and Steel Community wanted "to achieve a peace settlement primarily between France and Germany" (Dinan 2005: 2). Concerning this important goal, de Gasperi and his government were highly in favour for the ECSC. The other Italian political parties, however, hold a completely different view. Especially the Communist and Socialist party saw the Schuman Plan "as another aspect of America's growing hegemony in Europe" (Willis 1971: 36). As a consequence of this political dispute, the time between the treaty's signature and its ratification in 1952 was strongly affected by discussions between the governing Christian Democrats and the opposition parties (Mancini 2000: 128)

Evaluating the economic impact of the ECSC on Italy, it must be said that the country neither benefitted nor got negatively affected by it. Nevertheless, the political meaning behind this European alliance was extremely relevant. Italy was not only able to re-integrate itself within the European community, but also - due to de Gasperi's constant mediation between France and Germany - to secure a peaceful coexistence between those states (Dinan 2005: 4). As the Italian prime minister underlined after the successful ratification of the Schuman Declaration, his aim was a continuing unification of the European countries:

> "the future will not be built through force, nor the desire to conquer, but by the patient application of the democratic method, the constructive spirit of agreement, and by the respect for freedom."
>
> (De Gasperi 1952)

With the invasion of South Korea by Communist troops in 1950, the European integration process got an important new influence. Feeling now closely connected to the American side, the Italian government declared its support for the USA soon after the invasion. At that time, the European countries realized that a common defence alliance was necessary. Also in this case, especially De Gasperi, Sforza and Schuman sought to expedite the negotiation process between the other European countries. In February 1951, Italy, France, Germany, Belgium and Luxembourg came together for the "Paris Conference on the European Defence Community (EDC)" (Willis 1971: 43). Despite the immense efforts of persuading the other nations by de Gasperi and Schuman, most of the participants stayed sceptical towards this defence cooperation.

In June, shortly before he resigned as foreign minister, even Sforza feared that "the political ties of the Defence Community would make Italy economically vulnerable to the power of France and Germany by breaking its ties with the United States and Britain" (Willis 1971: 43). Also the Italian population was sceptical towards Italy's plan to join the European Defence Community.

The government's position, however, was clear: de Gasperi, who was now in charge of the foreign ministry, "committed himself fully and stubbornly to federalist ideals, and he was beginning to see the European Defence Community as the edifice that was to crown his life's work" (Willis 1971: 44). Therefore he intensified the negotiations with the other European countries. During the next year, the Italian foreign minister used many official meetings to argue exerted in favour of the EDC. By 1952, he signed the treaty for Italy. Driven by his successful commitment to a further European unification, de Gasperi soon after proposed together with Schuman the idea of a European Political Community (EPC). This project, however, faced a dramatic deadlock, as the ratification of the European Defence treaty ran into many difficulties. Especially in France and Germany, the strongest opponents within this alliance, the treaty was heavily criticised. Also the fact that France got a new foreign minister who "displayed much less interest than Schuman had in the cause of the European integration (…)", helped postpone presentation of the EDC treaty to the French Assembly (Willis 1971: 46/7).

The following year symbolized a miserable downfall for de Gasperi. During the election, his party tried to gain voters by underlining the important achievements for a European future during the last years. In clear opposition to that, the Communist and Socialist parties attacked de Gasperi and his policy sharply. In their opinion, Italy had worked toward a supranational political building that would endanger the Italian nation in the future (Di Nolfo 1980: 145). Obviously, many Italians shared this opinion, so de Gasperi lost the election. His ouster affected not only the national policy in Italy, but also the European integration process. Italy itself was struggling with national political difficulties and had to lay the ratification of the EDC treaty on ice. Other European countries also lost their believes in the common European alliance. In France, the French Assembly rejected the treaty only one year later. One event, however, gave hope for a common European future. At the London conference in late 1954, the new Italian foreign minister Gaetano Martino acted successfully as a mediator between the other European states. As a result of his commitment, Italy and Germany got admitted to the Brussels Pact and Germany became finally a member of the NATO (Willis 1971: 51).

Looking back at the period between 1949 and 1954, many political scientists and historians nowadays agree on the fact that it was "the high point of the Italian influence on the European integration process" (Dinan 2005: 2). Together with the French foreign minister, Alcide de Gasperi worked constantly for the successful European integration. Due to their efforts, they were called the founding fathers of Europe soon after the end of their political leadership (Di Nolfo 1980: 145).

4. 1954 - 1958: The milestone period of the European integration process

Despite all internal difficulties, the Christian Democratic Party didn't give up their aim of a persisting European integration. There were mainly three reasons that justified this behaviour. Firstly, the European integration appeared as a means by which Italy could be able to obtain foreign capital and therefore make sure a prosperous economic development (Calandri 2003: 511). Secondly, an extensive European integration was still seen as "a guarantee of international peace" (Willis 1971: 53). And finally, the multilateral alliance safeguarded a total integration for the Italian nation within the European community. In the following months Italy therefore initiated new negotiations between the European countries – first and foremost together with Germany,

France, and the Benelux states. At the end of these meetings, which were again successfully mediated and guided by the Italian government, the foreign ministers developed a draft framework for the European Economic Community (EEC). The key idea was to facilitate economic integration, to find a common social policy and to ensure a free movement of labour (Willis 1971: 55).

To continue the work on these ideas, the countries formed the Intergovernmental Committee of experts, the so-called Spaak Committee, which met for the first time in Brussels 1955 (Willis 1971: 56). The Italian government sent a really powerful delegation to this meeting, which was able to enforce the main Italian interest. And again, Italy acted as a wise mediator between France and Germany. Finally, the expert group agreed on three important concepts they discussed during the following month: a common European market, a community for atomic energy (EURATOM), and a sectoral integration of energy and transport (Dinan 2005). Several conferences followed where these concepts were intensively discussed. On the Venice Conference 1956, Italy was able to secure first concrete frameworks, which all the other states agreed upon (Willis 1971: 65). One year later, on the 25th of March 1957, the treaty for the Common Market as well as the EURATOM agreement was finally signed. This extraordinary ceremonial act took place on the Capitol Hill in Rome and symbolized the RILANCIO EUROPEO (the relaunching of Europe) (ibid.).

The city of Rome was not chosen coincidently for this historical celebration. It was the international appraisal for Italy's continuous dedication to a successful European integration during the last decade. The Italian government itself underlined at that day that "the new Europe would be the continuation of Rome – of the Republic and Empire, of the Christian Church, and of the Holy Roman Empire" (Willis 1971: 66). In October 1957, the Italian parliament ratified the Treaties of Rome – the success finale of more than 10 years of diplomatic efforts and at the same time the starting point for a prosperous European future.

5. Conclusion

"Europe has a history of instability and war; tying countries together politically and economically is a way to consolidate democracy and resolve the traditional causes of conflict." (Dinan 2005: 2)

As illustrated in this paper, the Italian nation played a significant role during the early European integration processes. More constantly than any other European country at that time, Italy tried to unify the European countries again after the disastrous event of the Second World War. The most influential person, who encouraged the integration process, was the Italian prime minister

Alcide de Gasperi. He committed his political life for this aim in order to recreate the peaceful coexistence of the European countries, to find a solution for the national and international fragmentations – regarding political as well as economical aspects, and to develop a future guideline for the European Union (Di Nolfo 1980: 164). Working closely together with the French foreign minister Robert Schuman, de Gasperi developed the early constitutional framework for the new Europe. Until today, he is therefore considered as one of the most important founding fathers of the European Union.

Also after the political ouster of de Gasperi in 1953, Italy continued his successful work towards a European integration. As a powerful mediator between the two strongest opponents, France and Germany, the Italian government found not only back to his inner state political stability but also to his equal international position among its European neighbour states. After the ratification of the Treaties of Rome in 1957, the Italian economical and political system benefitted immensely from the new established European Community.

Unfortunately, this auspicious period didn't last for a long time. During the First and Second Republic, the Italian attitude towards the European integration deteriorated and at the moment it looks like the Italian population is driven by scepticism and fear towards the European community" (Caciagli 2004: 30). Regarding the fact, however, that the new government under prime minister Matteo Renzi seems to renew the historical pro-European spirit of Alcide de Gasperi, political scientists should observe the future developments in Italy. Maybe the Italian population finds back to the European enthusiasm, which characterized the early years of the European integration process:

„Today there is the Council of Europe, tomorrow there will be an effective European union; today, there is a committe of ministers, tomorrow there will be a supernational organ of government; today there is a consultative assembly, tomorrow there must be a true and proper European parliament" (Alcide de Gasperi)

6. Bibliography

CACIAGLI, Mario, *Italien und Europa. Fortdauer eines Verhältnisses von Zwang und Ansporn*, in «Aus Politik und Zeitgeschichte», 2004, Berlin, Bundeszentrale für politische Bildung, S. 26-31.

CALANDRI, Elena, *Italy's Foreign Assistance Policy, 1959-1969*, in «Contemporary European History», Vol. 12, No. 4 (2003), pp. 509-525.

COMELLI, Michele, *Italy's Love Affair with the EU: Between Continuity and Change*, Rome, Istituto Affari Internazionale, Working papers 11/08, 2011, pp. 1-11.

DANIELS, Philip, *Italy in European Union*, in «Economic and Political Weekly», Vol. 33, No. 35 (1998), pp. 107-112.

DI NOLFO, Ennio, *Das Problem der europäischen Einigung als ein Aspekt der italienischen Außenpolitik 1945-1954*, in «Vierteljahrshefte für Zeitgeschichte», Vol. 28, No. 2 (1980), pp. 145-167.

DINAN, Desmond, *Ever Closer Union: An Introduction to European Integration*, Boulder, Lynne Rienner Publishers, 2005, pp. 1-8.

European Commission, *Alcide de Gasperi: an inspired mediator for democracy and freedom in Europe*. Online available at:

http://europa.eu/about-eu/eu-history/founding-fathers/pdf/alcide_de_gasperi_en.pdf

MANCINI, G. Frederico, *The Italians in Europe*, in «Foreign Affairs», Vol. 79, No. 2 (2000), pp. 122-134.

N24.de, *Matteo Renzi halt Plädoyer für Europa. "Mut zu radikalen Entscheidungen"*. Online available at :

http://www.n24.de/n24/Nachrichten/Politik/d/4336336/-mut-zu-radikalen-entscheidungen-.html

PEW Research Center, Washington, *The New Sick Man of Europe: the European Union. French Dispirited; Attitudes diverge sharply from Germans*, 2013. Online available at:

http://www.pewglobal.org/2013/05/13/the-new-sick-man-of-europe-the-european-union/

SPOTTS, Frederic, WIESER, Theodor, *Italy: A Difficult Democracy. A Survey of Italian Politics,* Cambridge, Cambridge University Press, 2005 (1986), pp. 263-291.

12

WILLIS, F. Roy, *Italy chooses Europe,* Oxford, Oxford University Press, 1971, pp. 12-29, 30-52, 53-71.